The **Joseph Rowntree Foundation** has supported this project as part of its programme of research and innovative development projects, which it hopes will be of value to policy makers, practitioners and service users. The facts presented and views expressed in this report are, however, those of the authors and not necessarily those of the Foundation.

Peter Beresford works with Open Services Project, is Professor of Social Policy, Brunel University, and is an active member of the Psychiatric System Survivors' Movement.

Tony Carter is a convenor of the Senior Citizens' Forums Network, former chair of the Greater London Forum for the Elderly, and is a pensioner involved in a number of pensioners' organisations.



Published for the Joseph Rowntree Foundation by YPS

ISBN 1 902633 81 4

Cover design by Adkins Design

Prepared and printed by:
York Publishing Services Ltd
64 Hallfield Road
Layerthorpe
York
YO31 7ZQ
Tel: 01904 430033 Fax: 01904 430868 E-mail: orders@yps.ymn.co.uk

There is no right way of involving the public. The choice of methods should be matched to the purpose and circumstances in which it takes place.

(Barker, Bullen, de Ville, 1999)

# Contents

# Acknowledgements

This report draws upon interviews and conversations with a considerable number of people. We would like to give our thanks for particular insights to the following:

| | |
|---|---|
| Alistair Beattie | Age Concern London |
| Suzy Croft | St John's Hospice/Open Services Project |
| Zelda Curtis | Older Women's Network UK |
| Stan Davison | Barnet Borough Senior Citizens' Forum |
| Andrew Dunning | Better Government for Older People Programme |
| Tessa Harding | Help the Aged |
| Jean McKay | Wiltshire and Swindon Users' Network |
| Nell McFadden | Strathclyde Elderly Forum |
| Caroline Nash | Researcher, Nottingham |
| Cecil Scholten | Consultant, Utrecht, the Netherlands |
| Barbara Scott | Community Health South London NHS Trust |
| Jan Stevenson | King's Fund |
| Margaret Winn | Age Concern Liverpool |
| Anne Wilson | Mental health service user/survivor |
| Roland Worth | Hunstanton Pensioners' Forum |

We would also like to thank Alex O'Neil of the Joseph Rowntree Foundation for his help in developing this report and the Joseph Rowntree Foundation for its financial support and practical commitment to the involvement of older people and other citizens in policy and practice.

We would like to give a particular thank you to members of the Joseph Rowntree Foundation's Older People's Programme Steering Group for their comments and ideas about our draft report, which we have tried to include in this final version.

# Summary

## Forms of involvement

This report examines a range of different but overlapping forms or models of involvement that have been developed to involve older people. These include:

1 advocacy and information
2 forums
3 user panels
4 consultation
5 user/pensioners' groups
6 user-led services
7 direct payments
8 networks
9 campaigning and direct action
10 initiatives in other countries

## Issues for involvement

Each approach has its strengths and weaknesses. Some work better in some circumstances and for particular purposes than others. But involvement is not just a matter of using different forms or techniques. It needs to be put in political, policy and personal context. Then we can get a clearer idea of what to expect from different forms and models of involvement and how to get the most out of them. To help do this, the report first looks at a number of key issues affecting the nature and effectiveness of involvement. Two helpful distinctions which emerge are between different philosophical approaches to involvement: *consumerist* and *democratic* approaches; and different sources for involvement: *agency-led* and *user/older people-led* initiatives. Again, each of these has its strengths and weaknesses. The issues explored in this part of the report include:

- current government and other initiatives for involving older people
- the background to involvement
- different approaches to/philosophies of involvement
- key components for effective involvement
- who and what involvement is actually for
- who controls involvement
- what we should expect from involvement
- issues of inclusion.

A number of characteristics for effective involvement emerge from these issues and it is hoped that these, taken together with information about specific different forms or models of involvement, will provide a basis for further discussion and action for older people and their organisations, as well as others committed to their involvement, at local and national level in working out practice and strategies for developing involvement.

## Issues for development

The report also details a number of specific examples of older people's involvement and identifies six key issues for the involvement of older people requiring more work and consideration. These are the following.

- The development of collective forms of involvement which are independently based and have the capacity to bring about change, but which are inclusive of as wide a range of older people as possible, including those who are physically and mentally frail (including older people with dementia), who communicate differently and whose mobility is restricted.
- Enabling as wide a range of older people as possible to be able to have more control over the individual support, services and professional input that they receive, to ensure it is as helpful, sensitive and appropriate as possible.
- In view of the lack of evidence of older people's and disabled people's groups and organisations working together in a major way, although older people make up the largest group of disabled people, exploring working relations between older and disabled people and their organisations to share and exchange their different knowledge, skills and experience, and encourage further collaboration.
- Exploring and supporting the involvement of black and minority ethnic older people in both user-led and agency-led arrangements to involve older people, in concert with black and minority ethnic elders and organisations.

- Supporting and maintaining the involvement of groups identified by social care, including people with learning difficulties, mental health service users and deaf people when they are older.
- Enabling and extending the involvement and say of older people in residential services.

# INTRODUCTION

> "I'm not sure older people like being 'organised'. That's why it's important to have the whole spectrum of involvement. Involvement is an individual thing, as well as a political and collective thing. Having control over your life matters, even if you don't want to organise things on a larger scale."
>
> (Members of the Steering Group of the Older People's Programme)

## Producing the report

This short report was originally commissioned by the Joseph Rowntree Foundation as part of the process of agenda setting for its Older People's Programme. We wrote a draft report to meet the brief set for us by the Older People's Programme Steering Group (made up of a majority of older people) and the Joseph Rowntree Foundation. We have drawn on our own experience and knowledge as an older person actively involved in the older people's movement and a psychiatric system survivor with experience as a writer, researcher and activist in the field of participation.

We have also spoken to a number of older people with experience and knowledge in this field. We had hoped in addition to organise a small meeting bringing together some additional older people and helpful allies, but, regrettably, time defeated us. This final draft of the report, however, does build on the comments and ideas of members of the Steering Group of the Older People's Programme at a meeting where they discussed our draft.

We have tried to write as clearly and accessibly as possible, avoiding jargon and initials, and we apologise where we may have failed. Participation is a field that is full of jargon and fancy terms. This may offer a helpful advance warning – that when it comes to getting involved, all may not be quite as it seems ...!

We should perhaps also say something about our own use of language and terminology. There is no agreed language in this field. Different people use different words to mean different things and, sometimes, special meanings are attached to words which other people may not be aware of. We have used the words participation and involvement or user involvement to describe the report's focus. We are using these words interchangeably to mean the same thing.

There is also no agreement about what is 'old' and 'older'. Some groups involve people from age 60 plus. Others have members who are much older. Old age can now span 20 or 30 years – or even more. This is another reason for avoiding stereotypes of older people and adopting as inclusive an approach as possible to involving older people, so that both 'older' and 'younger' older people have equal opportunities to be more involved if they wish to.

> "Ageing is a continuous process. We're all different. We want to get back into society."
>
> (Member of the Older People's Programme Steering Group)

## Aims of the report

The initial aim of this short report was to provide a brief guide to involvement for the Steering Group of the Older People's Programme as a basis for further work and discussion. We hope that it will now also be of wider use to older people and their organisations seeking to increase the say and involvement that they can have. The report is particularly concerned to offer a brief guide to different forms of participation so that older people and their organisations can:

- be as well informed as possible about the strengths and weaknesses of different models and approaches
- have a clearer idea of what they might be letting themselves in for when they get involved through any one of them
- choose the approach that best suits their requirements.

In our view, there is no one 'best value' form of older people's involvement and no reason to promote uniformity. Some of the forms for involvement developed by older people are unique to older people's organisations. As one member of the Steering Group of the Older People's Programme said:

> "Older people's organisations are all sorts of different animals. You can't change that. That's how it is."

# 1 Setting the scene

## 1 Putting older people's participation into context

There are three main reasons for putting a focus on participation. The first is that this Government places a big emphasis in its programmes and policy statements on participation and user involvement. It argues it wants:

- more open and participatory government
- to increase local democracy with more accessible and accountable local government
- partnerships with service users and other local people to ensure 'best quality' in its policies and services.

This has been reflected in the setting up of a vast number of consultations, focus groups, committees, forums, etc., to gather people's views. Conservative governments began this process. It is now happening even more with New Labour. This can be really helpful, but there can also be some real problems for people with this. If you or your group does not respond and 'get involved', then you may be ignored and louder more powerful voices may be listened to. But, if you do respond, you may use a lot of the limited amount of time, energy and resources which you have and neglect other possibly more important activities.

So, the first question about any invitation to get involved is *what is the cost benefit analysis*? What this means for people is looking for answers for the following questions.

- What are we really likely to get out of this?
- What will it actually cost us (in energy, time, skill and money)?
- Could we get more doing it differently?
- Should we be putting our efforts into other things?

The second reason for putting a focus on participation is that older people have frequently been marginalised and overlooked in initiatives for participation. Provision has not been made to ensure that they are fully included. This, combined with the lower demands and expectations that many people from older generations were encouraged to have, has restricted older people's involvement. Many older people face additional obstacles because of their low income, lack of access to transport, disability and the reduced confidence that can go with these.

The third reason for putting a focus on participation is that, because of the particular discriminations older people face on the basis of age, disability, sexuality and additionally gender (since the majority of older people, particularly very old people, are women), they have a long and strong tradition of developing *their own* organisations and initiatives to have more say and involvement and more control over their lives.

## Examples of involvement

**Nottinghamshire Elderly Voices**

Each year, the County Council calls a meeting. All older people's organisations are specifically invited but individuals are welcome to attend. An opening session of speeches, for instance by the Leader of the Council and perhaps a visiting speaker, leads to the presentation of an annual report based on the work of the Council relating to older people. Then, the audience breaks up into groups corresponding to the Council's committees, each group facilitated by staff members. Members of the group raise issues and discuss them, the outcome of discussion being noted by a staff member. These issues, collated, go to the appropriate council department and committee for consideration and form the basis of an annual report to the next annual meeting. Progress during the year is monitored by a group that includes representatives of local organisations of older people.

# 2 Being clear about involvement

The complicated context of participation is an important reason to get participation properly worked out – so that we can be sure we are clear about it and have the best possible idea of what it may and may not offer us, and when and where different forms of participation are likely to be helpful.

> "Consultation – it's all talk. It doesn't mean anything yet. Local authorities wouldn't know it if it hit them in the face. It does get very frustrating that consultation is a serious part of the process of democracy."
>
> (Member of the Older People's Programme Steering Group)

This also leads to a distinction that many people trying to get involved have found it helpful to make. This distinction is between:

- developing their own ideas and initiatives to get involved – and there are many different ways of doing this, as this report discusses – and
- responding to schemes set up by government, local authorities and service purchasers and providers to 'get involved'.

People are likely to have more control over the first, but the second may offer useful opportunities to influence official organisations. Also, official schemes for involvement often bring money with them, while it can be much more difficult to get money to do your own things. However, there may be restrictions on how you can spend this money. The best advice we have been given is to make sure we always spend more time on the first (our own initiatives for involvement) than the second (other people's)! Some useful questions to ask about any arrangement for involvement include the following.

- Who took the initiative?
- What is the objective?
- Who is on the management committee?
- Who decides the work programme and priorities?
- How is the initiative financed?
- How are decisions implemented?

> "Where we are, they are listening to us. It's like the water dripping on the stone. We have worked hard at it for years. It's taken a lot of effort."
>
> (Member of the Older People's Programme Steering Group)

## 3 Other initiatives for older people

The Government has introduced some specific initiatives for the involvement of older people. Its Better Government for Older People Programme was set up in 1998 'to promote the better coordination and responsiveness of public services and ... the recognition across Government that for too long older people's interests had been overlooked or undervalued'. It has a small unit of enthusiastic full-time staff and a steering committee that includes the Cabinet Office, the Local Government Association and a number of voluntary organisations concerned with older people. No organisation of older people is on the steering committee. Significantly, it was not until halfway through the two-year work of the programme, following strongly expressed views at a conference of older people involved in the work of the programme, that an older people's advisory group was set up.

The major part of the programme is 28 pilot projects 'experimenting with a more strategic, citizen centred, integrated approach than hitherto'. Approaches are varied and many of the pilot districts have successfully involved older people and their organisations.

The programme is also concerned to spread its message of effective involvement of older people and has set up a wider Learning Network for local authorities not involved; older people's organisations can join free. The programme has involved itself in other activities to encourage older people's inclusion, for instance it joined with the Department for Education and Employment in a conference on learning in later life.

Another government initiative is the establishment of an Inter-Ministerial Group on Older People, chaired by a Cabinet Office minister and bringing together ministers from all departments whose work has an impact on older people. This Group has been engaged in a 'listening programme' of visits throughout the country. Better Government for Older People also interacts with the Group.

In health, the interest in older people is somewhat mixed. Government policy includes accidents to older people as a priority area, but excludes them from specific action on heart disease, stroke and cancer. A National Standards Framework for older people is being prepared. It had the active involvement of an older people's reference group, now disbanded. (Its members have subsequently formed a campaigning group, Health and Older People.)

The work of the National Institute for Adult and Continuing Education in promoting its 'Older and Bolder' initiative for involvement in education is also relevant. The campaign has the full support of the University of the Third Age, a self-help learning group for older people.

Although the overall picture is patchy, there is some evidence of Government's intention to extend the involvement of older people. However, as yet in the UK, there is no national council or forum for older people as there is for women and some other groups.

The large national organisations for older people have also been active in this field. Age Concern has developed a policy for user involvement. Help the Aged developed its Speaking up for our Age programme. This involved regional and national events and provided funding for older people's groups to undertake their own activities.

## Examples of involvement

**Beth Johnson Foundation**
This foundation, based in Stoke on Trent, is a charitable trust working on projects involving older people, particularly on health issues – to use the phrase it minted, 'self-health'.

Among its projects is a Senior Health Shop based in Hanley – effectively the main centre of Stoke on Trent, an amalgam of six towns. The front of the shop is a 'healthy eating' cafeteria, providing a friendly way in, run by trained volunteers. They offer a bridge between the sociability of the shop and effective use of the comprehensive health-related information available.

Another project is Senior Citizens Involved in Public Services, Health and Advocacy. Project workers regularly visit small communities, such as a village or housing estate, over an extended period. Older people are encouraged in 'self-health' action and offered information, including access to advocacy and opportunities to discuss neighbourhood needs and services, particularly in terms of user friendliness. There is regular consultation with statutory and other agencies.

# 4 The background to involvement

### *An important health warning*

Before we move on to discuss particular approaches to participation, we would like to set out some general points to help make sense of these. We need to put schemes for involvement in context in this way because participation is not just about different techniques and methods of involving people.

A crucial thing to say about participation is that it is complicated, confusing and heavily political. It is essentially about power. This means that conflict, duplicity and possible heartache are never too far away. Nothing is certain about participation. There really aren't clear rules. Sometimes really unpromising schemes lead to something helpful and important. Other times, a well worked out initiative from an experienced users' organisation comes to nothing. As people who are already involved in older people's organisations will know from their own experience, there are no guarantees.

We are just trying to offer some additional guidance based on the experience of older people and other groups, as well as of supportive workers and organisations, to add to older people's own knowledge, to make the map a bit clearer.

## *Another health warning*

Most of us want to get involved to make a difference – to make something better for ourselves and for others, or to put right something that is wrong. Because of this, we get used to thinking of participation as a 'good thing'. We feel that we and other people should be doing it, and that official schemes for involvement are probably a good sign of commitment to service users and other local people's inclusion and interests. We also know it is more complicated that that. Schemes for involvement *do* have the potential to improve people's lives and make things more open and better. But, as well as having a *positive* or liberating potential, they also have a *negative* or regressive potential. We cannot just assume that the downside of participatory schemes is accidental and unfortunate. It crops up too often and needs to be included in people's calculations. Having just one older person, for example, on a committee or group, as often happens, is unlikely to be productive. The reality is that schemes for involvement can and do often serve as:

- a rubber stamp or window dressing for decisions that have really already been made to give an artificial appearance of involvement
- an unhelpful diversion from existing structures for accountability and democracy, like our local councillor, MP, etc., which may actually be more likely to get us the result we want
- a diversion from us putting our energy into our own ways of trying to bring about change
- a talking shop which is not actually connected to the decision-making process or which can be used to delay decision making.

To sum up, participatory schemes are not always a good thing and we should take account of this consideration when we are working out the most helpful kind of participation for any particular instance and how we can make the most effective use of our resources.

## 5 Different approaches to involvement

Two approaches to involvement have predominated in recent years. Nothing is clear-cut in participation and the approaches can merge into each other. But it is helpful to be able to distinguish between the two and not confuse them. The most common approach in state and service developments can best be described as a *consumerist* approach, while that developed by the citizens' and service users' movements and organisations can best be described as a *democratic* approach.

The consumerist approach to involvement, like consumerism more generally, is concerned with people as customers or consumers, buying goods and services. Involvement in this context is often about consultation to gather people's views to inform services so they can decide what *they* want to do for the future. It's like market research in ordinary businesses – asking your customers to improve your products and services to become more profitable.

The democratic approach is concerned with people having a say in decisions and in what happens to them. The consumerist approach does not mean any transfer in power or control. This is one of the key aims of the democratic approach.

## 6 Key components for involvement

Two components are essential to make involvement effective and inclusive, whatever model of involvement is adopted. These are: *access* and *support*. Without *support*, only the most confident, well-resourced and experienced individuals and groups are likely to get involved. Without *access*, efforts are likely to be difficult and ineffective, however assertive or skilled people are. *Access* means that people have ways into political, economic, social and welfare organisations, institutions and agencies that affect them so they can influence them. Such access extends from physical access to the availability of structures and arrangements that enable and encourage people's involvement. *Support* makes it possible for people to counter the obstacles and discrimination which they face. It includes:

- *support for personal development*: to increase people's confidence, assertiveness and expectations
- *support to develop skills*: to participate fully and effectively and on their own terms

- *practical support*: including information, advocacy, transport, payment and expenses
- *support for equal opportunities*: to ensure equal access, regardless of age, 'race', gender, sexuality, disability and communication differences
- *support to get together and work in groups.*

At present, few older people's organisations or groups have access to the resources to make such support possible and few agencies or service providers offer access in all its necessary forms.

## 7 Involvement for whom and for what?

The 1990s led to a massive expansion in what can be called *agency-led initiatives* for involvement. By this we mean official or 'non-user led' (for example, from the voluntary sector) initiatives and requests for people to get involved. An important example of this of significance to older people has been in the fields of social and community care. These schemes for involvement have been based mostly on a consumerist model of participation and have been concerned with improving the economy, efficiency and effectiveness of service purchasers and providers. Input from service users is particularly sought to help such agencies improve their operation. There has been an emphasis on involvement in the planning, management and running of services. As a result, there has been a great deal of such involvement, but the evidence of research and people's first-hand experience suggests that this has frequently *not* led to any appreciable improvement in the lives of people who got involved or in the availability, quality, adequacy or suitability of the support services they required. It has frequently resulted in service users acting as unpaid advisers and informants for services and then being criticised for being 'unrepresentative' when their views conflict with those of the services themselves. This raises a key question for would-be participants: who and what is their participation for? Do they want to get involved? Is it primarily:

1 To improve their lives, choices and opportunities and those of people like them? or
2 To make services and official organisations function better?

Most of us would generally answer *yes* to the first of these questions. It is helpful always to be clear what it is we are working for and whether the form of participation on offer or which we have selected is consistent with this.

It is important to be clear about who controls groups and organisations in which older people may get involved. The disabled people's movement has made a helpful distinction between organisations *for* disabled people and organisations *of* disabled people. By organisations *for* disabled people, they mean organisations controlled by non-disabled people. By organisations *of* disabled people, they mean organisations where control lies with disabled people themselves. This would mean, for example, that most or at least 51 per cent of the management group or committee were disabled people. This may also be a useful model and way of thinking for older people and their organisations.

## 8 Involvement: who controls it?

As we have already tried to stress and make clear, involvement can be a complex and subtle issue. As we have said, older people and their organisations can expect to be invited to take part in agency-led initiatives, like consultations and official committees. But official interest in involvement also extends to setting up older people's (and, indeed, mental health service users'/survivors' and disabled people's) groups and committees. This is important because it can create problems as well as opportunities. Thus, user groups come in a variety of guises – a spectrum ranging at one end from the user-controlled and managed, to agency-led initiatives and groupings of various kinds. Groups initiated by statutory or voluntary agencies usually have a pre-set objective or plan of work, for example to provide consultation on community care issues. The agency is naturally anxious to maintain that focus. On the other hand, older people who are involved may see important connections they want to make. Where the agency plays a more directive role – and this frequently happens – its concern to complete its own agenda may predominate.

> *Question*: "What do you see as the main health problem for older people in the area?"
>
> *Answer:* "Transport."
>
> (Group of older people involved in a health in later life campaign)

Of course, sometimes, older people and other groups are able to take control from agency-led initiatives and ensure that they pursue their concerns. Where management committees are less than majority controlled by older people, involvement becomes little more than consultation and, at one extreme, it can become tokenism. On the other hand, the involvement of professional workers who are not older is not necessarily bad; many older people-led groups and forums include such professionals. It should not be assumed that their interests are necessarily conflicting.

**Conversations with two older people involved in agency-led initiatives for involvement (neither willing to be identified)**
One was on an older people's committee set up by a local Council of Voluntary Service (CVS); the other in a similar committee established on the initiative of Age Concern with a community-care focus. In both cases, older people themselves were in a minority; most of the members were officers or professional workers from voluntary-sector organisations. One (CVS) said that there had been 'a tendency for the committee to pull its punches' with the Council because most of the organisations represented were funded by it. Lately, he detected a more 'militant' (his word) approach in the face of cuts to Council services because of financial restrictions. The other made similar comments: 'Age Concern is very wary of upsetting the Council because that's where its core funding comes from. That's true also of the Health Authority – a number of projects are set up with joint funding, although the Health Authority seems less touchy than the Council.'

Finance is a key issue here. Agencies, statutory and voluntary, usually prefer groups in which they can at least play some part. As a result, it tends to be these groups that receive grants and funding, while groups that assert their independence receive much less or nothing. It has to be recognised that democracy and involvement cost money and are not just for the 'respectable'!

A small voluntary-sector group for older people, encountered in the course of compiling this report, has an annual budget of £60,000, more than twice the expenditure of the entire 33 London senior citizens' forums.

## *Strengths and weaknesses of user-led and agency-led groups and initiatives*

### User-led initiatives

*Strengths* are:

- older people can determine their own agenda
- older people are in control
- independence
- user-led initiatives are more likely to have credibility with older people
- user-led initiatives are less likely to be swayed by the interests of the agency.

*Weaknesses* are:

- funding may be a problem
- lack of resources can restrict what the group can do and make it insecure.

### Agency-led initiatives

*Strengths* are:

- agency-led initiatives are more likely to gain funding and other official support
- they may have direct links with and routes into agencies
- official credibility.

*Weaknesses* are:

- older people's say may be limited
- official agendas tend to predominate
- they may be tokenistic.

Any conclusion on this subject runs the risk of itself being prescriptive. Perhaps the most that can be said is that a group initiated and run by older people themselves and responded to by decision makers in a positive way carries the possibility of leading to involvement in decision making. A group initiated by an agency, or even assisted by an agency, runs the risk of representing that agency's viewpoint, unless control is ceded to older people as soon as possible.

## 9 What we should expect from participation

> "You have to put yourself into a position with the Council where you can negotiate."
> (The late Les Stannard, Lewisham Pensioners' Forum)

Before we can be clear what kind of involvement we want to employ at any particular time or for any particular issue, we have to be clear what we see involvement as being *for*. This may be different for different people and groups and at different times. There is, however, a basic range of criteria which emerge repeatedly from older and other people's efforts to become more involved which certainly seem to help ensure effective and inclusive participation. These include the criteria listed below.

> "We need to stress the issue of urgency. How time is expired when you are older raises issues of time."
> (Member of Steering Group of Older People's Programme)

### ***Criteria for effective participation***

- access and support for people's involvement (see above)
- continuous opportunities for negotiation and agreement
- change linked with and following from people's involvement
- real improvements taking place as a result in people's life and services
- equality in involvement, so that all groups and individuals can be involved on equal terms
- challenging discrimination and securing people's human and civil rights
- participants being able to define their own criteria/ outcomes for participation.

It is helpful to measure past, present and future experiences of involvement against such a checklist. People will have their own, perhaps different, criteria to add.

## Examples of involvement

**Liverpool consumer groups**

In Liverpool, Age Concern has been running local consumer groups since the mid-1980s. It has nine Good Neighbour Offices, corresponding to the Council's social services district offices. There are six consumer groups which relate to the Good Neighbour Offices (a current reorganisation will reduce the number to five, corresponding to the areas of the newly established Primary Care Groups). Each local consumer group is composed of representatives from the day centres, lunch clubs and other older people's groups in the geographical area;

they elect a chairperson and other functions are carried out by Age Concern staff, with an officer of Age Concern Liverpool having overall responsibility.

The consumer groups act as an information exchange: between members, to and from Age Concern, city council services and other voluntary-sector organisations; to take up issues, either directly or passed upwards. An example might be the siting of a bus stop to improve convenience for attenders at a day centre. This could be dealt with directly with the city transport executive or passed to Age Concern head office.

Each local consumer group sends a representative to a Central Consumer Council, staffed by an Age Concern officer. This may deal with issues passed up by local groups but may also deal with larger issues raised by older people and appoint representatives to other bodies, including the local housing forum and the Joint Care Planning Team older people's subgroup.

Liverpool Age Concern is adamant that older people themselves control these groups; there is nothing to prevent the Central Consumer Council from taking a view different from that of Age Concern. A forum has now been set up in Liverpool, again at the initiative of Age Concern. The local consumer groups are represented.

## 10 Issues of inclusion

"Most structures involving older people are unfriendly to women, although increasingly women predominate in membership. Seating arrangements at meetings are

> confrontational, positions of power are held by men, discussions are inadequate and dominated by men."
> (Zelda Curtis, Older Women's Network, UK)

There is still much to be done to ensure the equal inclusion of women, black people and minority ethnic groups and other groups facing particular discrimination in older people's organisations. A 1992 study noted that most positions of power in pensioners' groups, including forums, were held by men (Carter and Nash, 1992). Often having a trade union background, these men had considerable organisational experience and a robust attitude to authority. In the years since, there seems to have been some change, but critics think that these changes are neither universal nor adequate. Further change may be on the way, though. At a recent National Pensioners' Convention meeting, Jay Ginn of Surrey University commented that the first generation of activists from the modern feminist movement was becoming pensioners. The traditional women's organisations, like the Women's Institutes and Townswomen's Guilds, with a largely older membership, also play some role and have great potential. Black and minority ethnic older people also seem to be under-represented in most pensioners' groups and participatory initiatives for older people. This may be because of earlier rebuffs in attempting to become involved in community organisations. In their working lives, they are likely to have played little part in their unions, if indeed they were in unionised employment, and were wary of joining or were unwelcome in other types of organisation. There is no powerful black elders' organisation. Where an existing pensioners' group makes efforts to involve them, the situation improves. The Greater London Forum for the Elderly and Lambeth Pensioners' Action Association are examples. The former has an active Black and Ethnic Minority

Elders Working Party and two black elders were voted on to the Forum's executive committee. There also seem to be obstacles in the way of the involvement of both younger and older old people generally, although more detailed information about this is not yet available.

> "More needs to be said about the way that women have been excluded from responsible positions in older people's organisations. We tend to accept that."
>
> (Older woman member of Steering Group of Older People's Programme)

## 11 Areas for involvement

While most schemes for involvement have been concerned with planning or managing policies and services, what has become clear recently are the possibilities for people to be involved in a much wider range of activities. Some of these also look like providing more fertile opportunities for involvement. Such areas include, for example, involvement in:

- the monitoring and evaluation of services
- professional education and training
- funding allocation and the setting of budgets
- defining and measuring social care standards and outcomes
- commissioning and undertaking research
- shaping, reviewing and regulating professional practice.

# 2 Models and forms of involvement

We now move on to the particular focus of this short report, different forms or models of participation. First, we should make clear that we have our own particular interests and our own biases. We have, however, tried to be as impartial as possible, although, as we have already tried to make clear, there is no neutrality in participation. In the short space available, we have had to generalise and some forms of involvement clearly overlap with others. We have tried to offer a brief discussion of each different model of involvement and set down some of their strengths and weaknesses. We realise we can describe only the tip of an iceberg. Our list of models and forms of involvement is not and could not be exhaustive.

We must also stress that we are not saying there is only one right way to be involved. Some people feel more comfortable with one model than another. The important point is that there is choice and it is often a matter of horses for courses. In the field of participation, nothing is totally predictable.

## 1 Advocacy and information

Advocacy and information are crucial for effective involvement and their availability is an essential part of getting involved successfully. We include them as key components of *support* for effective involvement.

Advocacy has mostly meant having someone to speak on your

behalf. More recently, the idea of *self-advocacy* has developed. This is used to mean learning to speak up for and getting involved *yourself*. Some service user groups have called themselves self-advocacy groups. Then, advocacy becomes a form of involvement.

There are different kinds of advocacy. These include legal (a lawyer), professional (like a social worker), lay (for example, an independent volunteer) and peer advocacy (provided by someone who has shared experience). Having an advocate can help people have a real say and become involved. On their own, they might not know how to do this or what they should say to help get their rights and entitlements. The evidence suggests that, to be really helpful, advocacy needs to be:

- independent: separate from services and service providers
- skilled: with advocates being suitably trained, supported and experienced
- accessible: provided in a suitable setting and going out to where people are, available at all times and not just in a crisis or when things have gone wrong.

It is important that advocacy should not be developed as an alternative to making agencies and services truly user-friendly, with the result that you have to have an advocate to get what you need. Also, all forms of advocacy should be geared to enabling people to work out what they want to do, rather than deciding for them. All forms of advocacy must always support self-advocacy.

Knowledge is power and reliable independent information is essential for effective involvement. This report reflects this. If older people are to get the most out of being involved, it is helpful to learn as much as possible from what other older people and their organisations have already discovered. The provision of information is also a key activity of older people's organisations. It makes it possible to share what people have learned, provides evidence for campaigns and helps to spread the word. Many older people's groups have newsletters and produce publications. The evidence suggests that, to be most helpful, information needs to:

1. be independent: separate from service agencies and providers and not tied to their values and assumptions
2. be clear, brief and of immediate relevance
3. match people's abilities, experience, knowledge, language and culture
4. take into account the particular needs of:
   - members of minority ethnic communities
   - people with limited mobility
   - people with sensory impairments
   - people with limited literacy skills
5. do the following:
   - link verbal and written information
   - be available from clear contact points
   - offer the chance to get to know the information-giver; people tend to place most trust in information from people they know.

The Internet and electronic mail provide new and important ways of both accessing information and making it more readily available to many people. A growing number of older people and older people's organisations are now getting connected up and this is likely to speed up as equipment becomes cheaper and charges are reduced.

### *Strengths*

- Advocacy and information are essentials for effective and broad-based involvement.
- They can increase people's confidence, assertiveness and knowledge.
- Self-advocacy – learning to speak for yourself – is a valuable stepping-stone to getting more involved.
- Advocacy – speaking up for older people – is an important activity of older people's organisations.

### *Weaknesses*

- Advocacy has often meant 'experts' speaking for older people and other groups, rather than helping them speak for themselves.
- Self-advocacy is sometimes taken to mean *speaking* for yourself rather than *acting* for yourself. It must mean both if positive changes are to happen.
- Information on its own is of little use. Do not confuse providing information with doing something. It has to be provided in suitable and effective ways and to be linked with action to make a difference.

## 2 Forums

Forums are the most widespread form of older people's involvement. There is a wide variety of forums. There are forums made up only of older people's organisations, only of individual members and of both. The older people's organisations that are involved are usually organisations controlled by older people, but they may sometimes also be organisations *for* older people, or for those with an interest in older people. In some cases, forums act as an umbrella of organisations *for* and not *of* older people. All forums share a common purpose – to make the voice of older people heard. They seek to find a wide base of support for involvement in local issues of concern to older people. They are *representative* organisations. There are now about 80 forums, most relating to a local authority area. (In Scotland, there are many locally or community-based forums.)

> "Senior Citizens' Forums give a voice to older people on things which concern them where they live. The particular needs and views of older people are often overlooked; a Forum can make sure their voice is heard."
> (Senior Citizens' Forums Network, Information Sheet)

Relationships between forums and local authorities vary. Some are very supportive, offering finance, office facilities and regular meetings. Others do no more than respond to submissions and a few actively discourage a forum preferring an agency-led consultative body. Forums take up a wide range of issues, including employment legislation changes (concern over the use of agency staff as care assistants), continuing and community care, pensions, sale of residential homes, etc. Many forums engage in public activity to seek a wider spread of older people's views or to test out ideas and policies.

**Examples of activities**

Barnet Forum held a conference with national speakers followed by workshops relating to health and social care, transport and housing, working and learning, and older people from black and minority ethnic groups. The speeches and the conclusions of the workshops were published. The forum committee concluded amongst other things that:

- the debate about older people is ... about values and attitudes ... the balance of choice with equity ... Dignity is the key word
- racism needs to be tackled
- education is vitally important ... Opportunities and resources need to be made available to allow this to be a life-long process ...

The umbrella organisation for most pensioners' groups, including senior citizens' forums, is the National Pensioners' Convention. This is a well-established organisation, assisted initially by the Trades Union Congress and by Age Concern England, with an office and a small staff and an affiliated membership of around two million. Because of its activity on pensions, it is sometimes seen as a single-issue organisation, but its council and committee minutes show a range of concerns, including recently the report of the Royal Commission on Long Term Care, several health issues, including preventive health and breast cancer, housing, transport and access issues and digital TV.

An officer of a newly founded forum, the founder of the eight-year-old Pensioners' Association, indicated to the authors that the new forum might involve more older people because the association was widely seen as a single-issue organisation (pensions).

### *Strengths*

- Forums can offer older people an effective focus for collective action and campaigning, connecting involvement at both grassroots and national levels.
- Forums are achieving an increasingly prominent profile for the voice of older people.
- In some cases, forums are achieving influence and changes in policy and practice.
- Forums can offer older people an independent voice.
- Forums are formally constituted representative organisations.

### *Weaknesses*

- Forums still come in for criticism because of the association of some of their activists with trade unionism and their traditional approach to involvement.
- Funding and resources continue to be problems for forums.
- Ensuring effective inclusion and equality continues to be a problem for many forums.

## 3 User panels

User panels have received a high profile in professional accounts of older people's involvement. 'The ways in which panels are recruited and constituted vary, as do their purposes. Generally panels are not constituted through sampling methods and are not intended to be representative of a population of users' (Thornton and Tozer, 1994). A well-known example of panels is the Fife Users' Panel. Age Concern Scotland set up seven user panels, each consisting of eight older and mainly frail service users (now supported by Fife Council). They articulate views about health and social care services through regular panel meetings and set their own agenda, for instance a sizeable amount of work on hospital discharge procedures.

### *Strengths*

- People who take part in panels seem to enjoy them and feel they are making a contribution.
- They can offer a snapshot of users' views at a point in time and as such can be useful in policy making, particularly *if* they are associated with other forms of older people's involvement.

### *Weaknesses*

- There are no guarantees that whoever runs a panel or receives its message will take any notice of what people say. The significant ability of panels to bring about improvements, either directly for their participants or more generally, has yet to be shown.
- When the membership of panels is very small, they are likely to command little interest or credibility.

- Panels are expensive to run, need constant maintenance and, if the effort cannot be sustained, they may result in disillusionment.

Age Concern Dudley has a 100 Panel aimed at people who are less mobile or not interested in attending meetings, although transport is provided for those who do wish to attend. Two questionnaires a year are sent out, with a less than 50 per cent response rate. Views are sought not only on service provision but also, for instance, on the Dudley Unitary Development Plan.

In Bromley, south-east London, the Council on Ageing, formed initially as part of the machinery of joint commissioning of community care, carried out a survey of older people in the borough. The questionnaire was developed in conjunction with other local organisations, including the local forum and disability organisations. It was completed by 682 older people and was a key element in developing a strategy. Those of the respondents who were willing have formed the basis of a permanent panel for which volunteers are being sought. The method and frequency of consultation have yet to be decided.

## 4 Consultation

Consultation is the form of involvement most commonly used officially. It can involve questionnaire surveys, public meetings, focus groups and a variety of other techniques. New approaches have also been developed in recent years, for example citizens' juries and electronic techniques using electronic mail and the Internet. Consultation is probably the form of involvement that service users, other citizens and their organisations have learnt to be most suspicious and wary of.

### *Strengths*

- Done well, consultation can draw in a very wide range of views, both individually and collectively, and provide valuable data for improving policy and practice.
- It can reach people individually as well as through groups.

### *Weaknesses*

- Participants have no guarantee that any notice will be taken of what they say. It takes time and energy to respond to consultation and, if nothing comes of it, it can be demoralising and damaging for both individuals and groups.
- Consultations tend to be shaped by and concerned with the interests and priorities of the agencies and services which set them up, rather than those of the people on the receiving end. This can make getting involved hard work, trying to pull them round to service users' interests and concerns.
- Consultations are often undertaken when planning is already developed and options or even preferred ways forward already identified.
- Because consultation can draw in a wide range of views, including those of individuals as well as groups, it can be used to sideline the controversial but valid views expressed by democratically constituted user groups.

## 5 User/pensioners' groups

User groups – that is to say, groups made up of people who use welfare state services – have developed on a massive scale in recent years. There are now groups for a wide range of service users and this includes older people's or pensioners' groups. There are local, regional, national and international groups. These groups are frequently formally and democratically constituted, with their own constitution, officers, structures and in some cases paid workers. They make it possible for people to gain skills, experience and confidence, to learn to work with others and to take collective action. They vary in their activities. Some have an active social component to their work. Most respond to campaigns initiated by the national older people's organisations. A growing number seek to intervene in local policy issues. Many local pensioners' groups are affiliated to the British Pensioners' and Trade Union Action Association.

### *Strengths*

- Pensioners' or older people's groups have all the strengths that come from doing things together with other people.
- They can offer individuals support and purpose, as well as, sometimes, social activities and contact, and they can also help them to gain new knowledge and skills.
- They offer a route into personal development as well as broader activities.
- They offer an effective way of people working out together what they want to do by developing their own agenda and then deciding for themselves how to carry it through.
- They also offer a starting point for connecting local with national issues through national federations and organisations.

### *Weaknesses*

- Many people are reluctant to get involved in groups. User groups are frequently under-resourced and have difficulty reaching out to involve as wide a range of people as they would wish, particularly members of minority ethnic groups.
- User groups are sometimes set up by non-service users, for example non-older people. When this happens, their independence and the degree to which older people are actually in control become unclear. This can be damaging and divisive.
- Being involved in a user or pensioners' group can be demanding, which may or may not be what an older person wants.

## 6 User-led services

User-led services, that is to say support services that service users play a central role in running and shaping, have attracted increasing interest in recent years. In some cases, user groups and organisations have set up their own user-controlled or user-led services; in others, they have been able to persuade mainstream service providers to increase the involvement of service users in their own services.

### *Strengths*

- Where services are more heavily influenced by service users, they tend to reflect service users' preferences more closely and provide what they want more closely.

- User-led services avoid waste and duplication because they are much less likely to result in inappropriate services that people do not want to use.

### *Weaknesses*

- There is considerable resistance to a strong user influence in many services and service agencies.
- General financial constraints can place serious limits on the degree to which services are able to be user-led.

## 7 Direct payments

The idea and practice of direct payments was pioneered by the disabled people's movement. It means that disabled people have direct control of finances and purchase their own package of support, hiring and firing their own personal assistants. They decide on what kind of support they want and when and who provides it. The idea is for recipients of direct payments to receive assistance from local organisations controlled by service users.

### *Strengths*

- Research by disabled people indicates that people with direct payments are particularly satisfied with the support they receive.
- Direct payments put people in overall control of their services/support and effectively 'cut out the middle man'.
- With suitable support, information and advice from local service user organisations, it looks as though almost anyone could benefit from direct payments.

### *Weaknesses*

- So far, older people have not been included in legislation for direct payments. Further government action is expected and it is likely that at least some older people will be eligible in the future.
- The imposition of individual cash limits/ceilings restricts the support to which people are entitled, with adverse effects.
- Government has yet to offer adequate funding to service user organisations to support direct payments schemes and there has been a widespread lack of enthusiasm from local authorities for direct payments because of the competition they represent to their role as a service providers.
- Some older people worry that they could not manage or cope with employing someone, even with support.
- Traditional professionals, who tend to think of service users in terms of what they can't do rather than what they can do, are still likely to be involved in the assessment process, sometimes bringing to it an approach based on highlighting older people's deficits rather than their abilities.

## 8 Networks

An approach to involvement that takes the idea of user groups a step further is that of networks. These tend to include a range of different service users, for example older and disabled people, people with learning difficulties and mental health service users/ survivors. They also tend to operate at county or regional level, feeding into and linking with local service providers.

Wiltshire and Swindon Users' Network's objective is to 'promote user involvement in community care purchasing, provision and evaluation' (Mission Statement). The Network was set up about seven years ago and, with both individuals and organisations in the membership, has expanded the scope of its work. It now has 25 paid workers, including six full-time. It involves and works with a wide range of groups and service users, including older people. Funding comes from social services, health authorities and donations.

Its activities fall into two broad categories: development work and projects. Development work is geographically based, with a worker in each area. The work is varied and includes working with groups of people, meetings with statutory agencies, passing on views of groups to service providers and training. Examples include working with a disability forum in Swindon; working with professionals in Salisbury to write a self-harm policy; starting a cyber cafe for disabled people in Trowbridge; working with a mental health forum in Malmesbury. Not all the activity is community care or narrowly defined health. The 1998/99 annual report refers to work on transport issues and adult education.

There are currently five projects supported by joint finance, three developing advocacy work, two direct payments and transport in North and West Wiltshire. Other work includes a housing group, a social services inspection advisory panel, meetings about changing policy, meetings of service users with social services committee members and training.

### *Strengths*

- Networks can be an effective way of developing and maintaining involvement at regional and county level, while maintaining local links.

- They are invaluable in forging links, alliances and understanding between different groups of social care service users, which makes it much more difficult for agencies and services to play them off against each other.
- They can be independent but can also maintain close links and good communication with official agencies.
- They make it possible for groups like older people and mental health service users to learn from each other's experience and to develop new skills and ways of working.

### *Weaknesses*

- Links with service providers, particularly financial links and dependence, can weaken the independence of such networks.
- Networks are sometimes seen as an alternative to fully independent user groups by local authorities and services and are set up accordingly as a safer alternative.

## 9 Campaigning and direct action

Campaigning and direct action may take a variety of forms. They may include demonstrations, pickets, marches, media events and so on. Campaigning and direct action can be based on a *conflict-* rather than *consensus*-based form of involvement. When no door is open, they represent a form of banging on the door – of officialdom and authority. They represent a form of involvement that may be used by people as part of another form, for example by forums or user groups as part of their campaigning activity. Pensioners' groups and senior citizen forums are both actively involved in campaigning, which sometimes includes direct action. The older people's, disabled people's and mental health service users' movements have all developed forms of campaigning and direct action which take account of the particular circumstances and abilities of their members and are based on suitable and accessible forms of involvement.

> "Campaigning is involvement."
> (Joe Simmons, President of the British Pensioners and Trade Union Action Association and active campaigner on local issues)

### *Strengths*

- Campaigning and direct action can be very effective in bringing about change, especially when they are properly linked with media and other forms of activity.
- They can generate among those taking part strong feelings of solidarity and strength, which have a lasting effect beyond the immediate situation.

### *Weaknesses*

- Some people are unhappy with the conflict and confrontation that can be part of campaigning and direct action.
- Direct action can lead to hostility, arrest and even violence.

> "There wasn't a pedestrian crossing. We sat in the road. Two weeks later there was a crossing. I thought it was very good. It was encouraging. This is what could happen."
> (Member of the Steering Group of the Older People's Programme)

## 10 Initiatives in other countries

There are equivalents of forums elsewhere in Europe. These are senior councils and they are common in Scandinavia, the Netherlands, Belgium and Germany and are growing in number in Italy and Spain. (In France, a somewhat similar structure exists, relating to the local government structure.) Senior councils exist by law in Denmark and Norway, with a legal right of reply to representations; elsewhere, they receive official encouragement.

**The Netherlands**
There are some 500 municipalities, 280 of them with senior councils. A national network holds an annual conference every two years. The network is to be government funded. It runs Seniorweb, a website on older issues, financed by the Government, the state bank and the telecommunications corporation. An Internet network of senior councils is being set up. The senior councils include the local branches of the three main pensioners' national organisations (two religious, one secular) and welfare organisations, also mainly denominational; their competence includes any issue appropriate to the local authority (information from an unpublished paper by Cecil Scholten, Utrecht).

# 3 Issues for further exploration

Existing experience highlights the importance of forms of involvement that have some potential for bringing about real and direct changes and improvements in people's lives and the conditions in which they live. It also places some large question marks over agency-led initiatives for involvement. New forms of involvement are developing. Indeed, older people are among those developing them. There does seem to be a tension between effectiveness and inclusion with different forms of participation. For example, small and experienced user groups can be very effective and so can direct action, but both can leave out a lot of people. On the other hand, consultative arrangements can draw in a wide range of views but can then be ignored or used to legitimate an agency's own pre-set agenda. From this initial work, we have identified some possible priorities that older people's organisations (as well as policy makers and funders) may want to consider and use to inform their own priorities for action.

## Suggested priorities

More work is required on collective forms of involvement which are independently based and have the capacity to bring about change, but which are inclusive of as wide a range of older people as possible, including those who are physically and mentally frail (including older people with dementia), communicate differently and whose mobility is restricted.

At another level, more work is required on enabling as wide a range of older people as possible to be able to have more control over the individual support, services and professional input that they receive, to ensure it is as helpful, sensitive and appropriate as possible.

We have also been struck by the lack of evidence of older people's and disabled people's groups and organisations working together in a major way. Bearing in mind the fact that older people make up the largest group of disabled people, further work to explore working relations between older and disabled people and their organisations to share and exchange their different knowledge, skills and experience is likely to be helpful.

There is clearly more work needing to be done to explore and support the involvement of black and minority ethnic older people in both user-led and agency-led arrangements to involve older people. This clearly needs to be done in concert with black and minority ethnic organisations, elders and organisations like the REU (Race Equality Unit).

Groups identified by social care, like people with learning difficulties, mental health service users and people with physical and sensory impairments, face additional issues and challenges as they grow older. More work needs to be done to support and maintain their involvement to ensure that they can participate on equal terms with other older people, and that difficulties and discriminations which they have experienced are not reinforced as they become older.

While most older people live in their own homes, a large number do enter residential services. The nature and quality of such provision vary enormously, but living in residential services raises particular issues and problems in ensuring that people have the choices, opportunities and say that may be taken for granted when they are living independently.

# Resources

We have drawn on a number of reports, books and other material in preparing this report. We include details below. This list is not intended to be exhaustive, but it will hopefully be helpful for people seeking further information on this subject.


Barker, J., Bullen, M. and de Ville, J. (1999) *Reference Manual for Public Involvement.* Bromley Health, West Kent Health Authority, Lambeth, Southwark and Lewisham Health Authority

Beresford, P. and Croft, S. (1993) *Citizen Involvement: A Practical Guide for Change.* Macmillan

Better Government for Older People Programme (1999) *Making it Happen: Report of the First Year of the Programme.* (See also the occasional bulletin of the Programme, *Strategem.*) Cabinet Office

Carter, T. and Nash, C. (1992) *Pensioners' Forums: An Active Voice, The First Study of Senior Citizens' Forums.* Pre-retirement Association

Carter, T. and Nash, C. (2000) *Senior Citizens' Forums: A Guide to Get you Started.* Help the Aged and National Pensioners' Convention

Croft, S. and Beresford, P. (1993) *Getting Involved: a Practical Manual.* Open Services Project

Dunning, A. (1998) 'Advocacy, empowerment and older people', in M. Bernard and J. Phillips (eds) *The Social Policy of Old Age: Moving into the 21st Century.* Centre for Policy on Ageing

Dunning, A. (1999) 'The participation of older people in policy making', *Generations Review, Journal of the British Society of Gerontology,* Vol. 9, No. 4, December, p. 19

Evers, A. (1996) 'Traditions, changes and innovations in the representation of the elderly: status reports from five EU countries', paper presented at a conference in Bonn, Germany

Greater London Forum for the Elderly (2000) *Annual Report, 1999–2000.* Greater London Forum for the Elderly

Harding, T. and Oldman, H. (1996) *Involving Service Users and Carers in Local Services*. National Institute for Social Work and Surrey County Council

Help the Aged (1999) *Speaking up for our Age: Report of a Series of Regional Conferences to Encourage the Setting up of Forums*. Help the Aged

Jack, R. (ed.) (1995) *Empowerment in Community Care*. Chapman and Hall

Kelly-Lyth, M. and Leslie, S. (1999) 'Older people: new times – meeting the challenge', report of a conference hosted by Barnet Borough Senior Citizens' Forum. Barnet Senior Citizens' Forum

Lindow, V. and Morris, J. (1995) *Service User Involvement: Synthesis of Findings and Experience in the Field of Community Care*. Joseph Rowntree Foundation

National Pensioners' Convention (various dates) Newsletter and information sheets

Palfrey, S. (1994) *The Older Voice in Community Care: Planning and Provision*. Greater London Forum for the Elderly

Senior Citizens' Forums Network (various dates) Information sheets, occasional bulletins and other publications

Shaping Our Lives (1998) *Shaping Our Lives: the Video*. National Institute for Social Work

Thornton, P. and Tozer, R. (1994) *Involving Older People in Planning and Evaluating Community Care: a Review of Initiatives*. Social Policy Research Unit, University of York

Thornton, P. and Tozer, R. (1995) *Having a Say in Change: Older People and Community Care*. Community Care into Practice series. Community Care/Joseph Rowntree Foundation

Wiltshire and Swindon Users' Network (1999) *Seventh Annual Report, 1998–99*